The Three Billy Goats Gruff

Written by Emily Clark
Illustrated by Polly Jordan

The three Billy Goats Gruff
wanted to cross Troll's bridge
because the grass was
greener on the other side.

First went the littlest
Billy Goat Gruff.
Trip, trap, trip, trap, trip, trap.

"Who dares to cross my bridge?"

"It's me, the littlest
Billy Goat Gruff.
Don't eat me. My big
brother is close behind."

"Next went the middle-sized
Billy Goat Gruff.
Trip, trap, trip, trap, trip, trap.

"Who dares to cross my bridge?"

"It's me, the middle-sized
Billy Goat Gruff."

Don't eat me. My big
brother is close behind."

**After a while went
Big Billy Goat Gruff.**

Trip, trap, trip, trap, trip, trap.

"Who dares to cross my bridge?"

"It's me, Big Billy Goat Gruff.
Eat me if you think you can."

The Troll leaped up on
the bridge and charged
Big Brother Billy.

Big Goat Gruff lowered his great horns and...

butted Troll right off the bridge.